U. S. Small Business Administration

Table of Small Business Size Standards

Matched to

North American Industry Classification System Codes

This table lists small business size standards matched to industries described in the North American Industry Classification System (NAICS), as modified by the Office of Management and Budget effective January 1, 2012. The latest NAICS codes are referred to as NAICS 2012.

The size standards are for the most part expressed in either millions of dollars (those preceded by "$") or number of employees (those without the "$"). A size standard is the largest that a concern can be and still qualify as a small business for Federal Government programs. For the most part, size standards are the average annual receipts or the average employment of a firm. How to calculate average annual receipts and average employment of a firm can be found in 13 CFR § 121.104 and 13 CFR § 121.106, respectively.

SBA also includes the table of size standards in the Small Business Size Regulations, 13 CFR § 121.201. This table includes size standards that have changed since the last publication of 13 CFR § 121.

For more information on these size standards, please visit *http://www.sba.gov/size*.

If you have any other questions concerning size standards, contact a Size Specialist at your nearest SBA Government Contracting Area Office (list at the end of the table), or contact the Office of Size Standards by email at *sizestandards@sba.gov* or by phone at (202) 205-6618.

These size standards are effective January 7, 2013

NAICS Codes	NAICS Industry Description	Size Standards in millions of dollars	Size standards in number of employees
	Sector 11 – Agriculture, Forestry, Fishing and Hunting		
	Subsector 111 – Crop Production		
111110	Soybean Farming	$0.75	
111120	Oilseed (except Soybean) Farming	$0.75	
111130	Dry Pea and Bean Farming	$0.75	
111140	Wheat Farming	$0.75	
111150	Corn Farming	$0.75	
111160	Rice Farming	$0.75	
111191	Oilseed and Grain Combination Farming	$0.75	
111199	All Other Grain Farming	$0.75	
111211	Potato Farming	$0.75	
111219	Other Vegetable (except Potato) and Melon Farming	$0.75	
111310	Orange Groves	$0.75	
111320	Citrus (except Orange) Groves	$0.75	
111331	Apple Orchards	$0.75	
111332	Grape Vineyards	$0.75	
111333	Strawberry Farming	$0.75	
111334	Berry (except Strawberry) Farming	$0.75	
111335	Tree Nut Farming	$0.75	
111336	Fruit and Tree Nut Combination Farming	$0.75	
111339	Other Noncitrus Fruit Farming	$0.75	
111411	Mushroom Production	$0.75	
111419	Other Food Crops Grown Under Cover	$0.75	
111421	Nursery and Tree Production	$0.75	
111422	Floriculture Production	$0.75	
111910	Tobacco Farming	$0.75	
111920	Cotton Farming	$0.75	
111930	Sugarcane Farming	$0.75	
111940	Hay Farming	$0.75	
111991	Sugar Beet Farming	$0.75	
111992	Peanut Farming	$0.75	
111998	All Other Miscellaneous Crop Farming	$0.75	
	Subsector 112 – Animal Production and Aquaculture		
112111	Beef Cattle Ranching and Farming	$0.75	
112112	Cattle Feedlots	$2.0	
112120	Dairy Cattle and Milk Production	$0.75	

NAICS Codes	NAICS Industry Description	Size Standards in millions of dollars	Size standards in number of employees
112210	Hog and Pig Farming	$0.75	
112310	Chicken Egg Production	$12.5	
112320	Broilers and Other Meat Type Chicken Production	$0.75	
112330	Turkey Production	$0.75	
112340	Poultry Hatcheries	$0.75	
112390	Other Poultry Production	$0.75	
112410	Sheep Farming	$0.75	
112420	Goat Farming	$0.75	
112511	Finfish Farming and Fish Hatcheries	$0.75	
112512	Shellfish Farming	$0.75	
112519	Other Aquaculture	$0.75	
112910	Apiculture	$0.75	
112920	Horses and Other Equine Production	$0.75	
112930	Fur-Bearing Animal and Rabbit Production	$0.75	
112990	All Other Animal Production	$0.75	
Subsector 113 – Forestry and Logging			
113110	Timber Tract Operations	$7.0	
113210	Forest Nurseries and Gathering of Forest Products	$7.0	
113310	Logging		500
Subsector 114 – Fishing, Hunting and Trapping			
114111	Finfish Fishing	$4.0	
114112	Shellfish Fishing	$4.0	
114119	Other Marine Fishing	$4.0	
114210	Hunting and Trapping	$4.0	
Subsector 115 – Support Activities for Agriculture and Forestry			
115111	Cotton Ginning	$7.0	
115112	Soil Preparation, Planting, and Cultivating	$7.0	
115113	Crop Harvesting, Primarily by Machine	$7.0	
115114	Postharvest Crop Activities (except Cotton Ginning)	$7.0	
115115	Farm Labor Contractors and Crew Leaders	$7.0	
115116	Farm Management Services	$7.0	
115210	Support Activities for Animal Production	$7.0	
115310	Support Activities for Forestry	$7.0	
Except,	Forest Fire Suppression[17]	$17.5[17]	
Except,	Fuels Management Services[17]	$17.5[17]	

NAICS Codes	NAICS Industry Description	Size Standards in millions of dollars	Size standards in number of employees
Sector 21 – Mining, Quarrying, and Oil and Gas Extraction			
**Subsector 211 – Oil and Gas Extraction**			
211111	Crude Petroleum and Natural Gas Extraction		500
211112	Natural Gas Liquid Extraction		500
**Subsector 212 – Mining (except Oil and Gas)**			
212111	Bituminous Coal and Lignite Surface Mining		500
212112	Bituminous Coal Underground Mining		500
212113	Anthracite Mining		500
212210	Iron Ore Mining		500
212221	Gold Ore Mining		500
212222	Silver Ore Mining		500
212231	Lead Ore and Zinc Ore Mining		500
212234	Copper Ore and Nickel Ore Mining		500
212291	Uranium-Radium-Vanadium Ore Mining		500
212299	All Other Metal Ore Mining		500
212311	Dimension Stone Mining and Quarrying		500
212312	Crushed and Broken Limestone Mining and Quarrying		500
212313	Crushed and Broken Granite Mining and Quarrying		500
212319	Other Crushed and Broken Stone Mining and Quarrying		500
212321	Construction Sand and Gravel Mining		500
212322	Industrial Sand Mining		500
212324	Kaolin and Ball Clay Mining		500
212325	Clay and Ceramic and Refractory Minerals Mining		500
212391	Potash, Soda, and Borate Mineral Mining		500
212392	Phosphate Rock Mining		500
212393	Other Chemical and Fertilizer Mineral Mining		500
212399	All Other Nonmetallic Mineral Mining		500
**Subsector 213 – Support Activities for Mining**			
213111	Drilling Oil and Gas Wells		500
213112	Support Activities for Oil and Gas Operations	$7.0	
213113	Support Activities for Coal Mining	$7.0	
213114	Support Activities for Metal Mining	$7.0	
213115	Support Activities for Nonmetallic Minerals (except Fuels)	$7.0	

NAICS Codes	NAICS Industry Description	Size Standards in millions of dollars	Size standards in number of employees
	Sector 22 – Utilities		
	Subsector 221 – Utilities		
221111	Hydroelectric Power Generation	4 million megawatt hours[1]	
221112	Fossil Fuel Electric Power Generation	4 million megawatt hours[1]	
221113	Nuclear Electric Power Generation	4 million megawatt hours[1]	
221114	Solar Electric Power Generation	4 million megawatt hours[1]	
221115	Wind Electric Power Generation	4 million megawatt hours[1]	
221116	Geothermal Electric Power Generation	4 million megawatt hours[1]	
221117	Biomass Electric Power Generation	4 million megawatt hours[1]	
221118	Other Electric Power Generation	4 million megawatt hours[1]	
221121	Electric Bulk Power Transmission and Control	4 million megawatt hours[1]	
221122	Electric Power Distribution	4 million megawatt hours[1]	
221210	Natural Gas Distribution		500
221310	Water Supply and Irrigation Systems	$7.0	
221320	Sewage Treatment Facilities	$7.0	
221330	Steam and Air-Conditioning Supply	$12.5	

NAICS Codes	NAICS Industry Description	Size Standards in millions of dollars	Size standards in number of employees
Sector 23 – Construction			
Subsector 236 – Construction of Buildings			
236115	New Single-family Housing Construction (Except For-Sale Builders)	$33.5	
236116	New Multifamily Housing Construction (except For-Sale Builders)	$33.5	
236117	New Housing For-Sale Builders	$33.5	
236118	Residential Remodelers	$33.5	
236210	Industrial Building Construction	$33.5	
236220	Commercial and Institutional Building Construction	$33.5	
Subsector 237 – Heavy and Civil Engineering Construction			
237110	Water and Sewer Line and Related Structures Construction	$33.5	
237120	Oil and Gas Pipeline and Related Structures Construction	$33.5	
237130	Power and Communication Line and Related Structures Construction	$33.5	
237210	Land Subdivision	$7.0	
237310	Highway, Street, and Bridge Construction	$33.5	
237990	Other Heavy and Civil Engineering Construction	$33.5	
Except,	Dredging and Surface Cleanup Activities[2]	$20.0[2]	
Subsector 238 – Specialty Trade Contractors			
238110	Poured Concrete Foundation and Structure Contractors	$14.0	
238120	Structural Steel and Precast Concrete Contractors	$14.0	
238130	Framing Contractors	$14.0	
238140	Masonry Contractors	$14.0	
238150	Glass and Glazing Contractors	$14.0	
238160	Roofing Contractors	$14.0	
238170	Siding Contractors	$14.0	
238190	Other Foundation, Structure, and Building Exterior Contractors	$14.0	
238210	Electrical Contractors and Other Wiring Installation Contractors	$14.0	
238220	Plumbing, Heating, and Air-Conditioning Contractors	$14.0	
238290	Other Building Equipment Contractors	$14.0	
238310	Drywall and Insulation Contractors	$14.0	

NAICS Codes	NAICS Industry Description	Size Standards in millions of dollars	Size standards in number of employees
238320	Painting and Wall Covering Contractors	$14.0	
238330	Flooring Contractors	$14.0	
238340	Tile and Terrazzo Contractors	$14.0	
238350	Finish Carpentry Contractors	$14.0	
238390	Other Building Finishing Contractors	$14.0	
238910	Site Preparation Contractors	$14.0	
238990	All Other Specialty Trade Contractors[13]	$14.0[13]	
Sector 31 – 33 – Manufacturing			
Subsector 311 – Food Manufacturing			
311111	Dog and Cat Food Manufacturing		500
311119	Other Animal Food Manufacturing		500
311211	Flour Milling		500
311212	Rice Milling		500
311213	Malt Manufacturing		500
311221	Wet Corn Milling		750
311224	Soybean and Other Oilseed Processing		1,000
311225	Fats and Oils Refining and Blending		1,000
311230	Breakfast Cereal Manufacturing		1,000
311313	Beet Sugar Manufacturing		750
311314	Cane Sugar Manufacturing		750
311340	Nonchocolate Confectionery Manufacturing		500
311351	Chocolate and Confectionery Manufacturing from Cacao Beans		500
311352	Confectionery Manufacturing from Purchased Chocolate		500
311411	Frozen Fruit, Juice and Vegetable Manufacturing		500
311412	Frozen Specialty Food Manufacturing		500
311421	Fruit and Vegetable Canning[3]		500[3]
311422	Specialty Canning		1,000
311423	Dried and Dehydrated Food Manufacturing		500
311511	Fluid Milk Manufacturing		500
311512	Creamery Butter Manufacturing		500
311513	Cheese Manufacturing		500
311514	Dry, Condensed, and Evaporated Dairy Product Manufacturing		500
311520	Ice Cream and Frozen Dessert Manufacturing		500
311611	Animal (except Poultry) Slaughtering		500

NAICS Codes	NAICS Industry Description	Size Standards in millions of dollars	Size standards in number of employees
311612	Meat Processed from Carcasses		500
311613	Rendering and Meat Byproduct Processing		500
311615	Poultry Processing		500
311710	Seafood Product Preparation and Packaging		500
311811	Retail Bakeries		500
311812	Commercial Bakeries		500
311813	Frozen Cakes, Pies, and Other Pastries Manufacturing		500
311821	Cookie and Cracker Manufacturing		750
311824	Dry Pasta, Dough, and Flour Mixes Manufacturing from Purchased Flour		500
311830	Tortilla Manufacturing		500
311911	Roasted Nuts and Peanut Butter Manufacturing		500
311919	Other Snack Food Manufacturing		500
311920	Coffee and Tea Manufacturing		500
311930	Flavoring Syrup and Concentrate Manufacturing		500
311941	Mayonnaise, Dressing and Other Prepared Sauce Manufacturing		500
311942	Spice and Extract Manufacturing		500
311991	Perishable Prepared Food Manufacturing		500
311999	All Other Miscellaneous Food Manufacturing		500
Subsector 312 – Beverage and Tobacco Product Manufacturing			
312111	Soft Drink Manufacturing		500
312112	Bottled Water Manufacturing		500
312113	Ice Manufacturing		500
312120	Breweries		500
312130	Wineries		500
312140	Distilleries		750
312230	Tobacco Manufacturing		1,000
Subsector 313 – Textile Mills			
313110	Fiber, Yarn, and Thread Mills		500
313210	Broadwoven Fabric Mills		1,000
313220	Narrow Fabric Mills and Schiffli Machine Embroidery		500
313230	Nonwoven Fabric Mills		500
313240	Knit Fabric Mills		500
313310	Textile and Fabric Finishing Mills		1,000
313320	Fabric Coating Mills		1,000

NAICS Codes	NAICS Industry Description	Size Standards in millions of dollars	Size standards in number of employees
Subsector 314 – Textile Product Mills			
314110	Carpet and Rug Mills		500
314120	Curtain and Linen Mills		500
314910	Textile Bag and Canvas Mills		500
314994	Rope, Cordage, Twine, Tire Cord, and Tire Fabric Mills		1,000
314999	All Other Miscellaneous Textile Product Mills		500
Subsector 315 – Apparel Manufacturing			
315110	Hosiery and Sock Mills		500
315190	Other Apparel Knitting Mills		500
315210	Cut and Sew Apparel Contractors		500
315220	Men's and Boys' Cut and Sew Apparel Manufacturing		500
315240	Women's, Girls', and Infants' Cut and Sew Apparel Manufacturing		500
315280	Other Cut and Sew Apparel Manufacturing		500
315990	Apparel Accessories and Other Apparel Manufacturing		500
Subsector 316 – Leather and Allied Product Manufacturing			
316110	Leather and Hide Tanning and Finishing		500
316210	Footwear Manufacturing		1,000
316992	Women's Handbag and Purse Manufacturing		500
316998	All Other Leather Good and Allied Product Manufacturing		500
Subsector 321 – Wood Product Manufacturing			
321113	Sawmills		500
321114	Wood Preservation		500
321211	Hardwood Veneer and Plywood Manufacturing		500
321212	Softwood Veneer and Plywood Manufacturing		500
321213	Engineered Wood Member (except Truss) Manufacturing		500
321214	Truss Manufacturing		500
321219	Reconstituted Wood Product Manufacturing		500
321911	Wood Window and Door Manufacturing		500
321912	Cut Stock, Resawing Lumber, and Planing		500
321918	Other Millwork (including Flooring)		500
321920	Wood Container and Pallet Manufacturing		500
321991	Manufactured Home (Mobile Home) Manufacturing		500

NAICS Codes	NAICS Industry Description	Size Standards in millions of dollars	Size standards in number of employees
321992	Prefabricated Wood Building Manufacturing		500
321999	All Other Miscellaneous Wood Product Manufacturing		500
Subsector 322 – Paper Manufacturing			
322110	Pulp Mills		750
322121	Paper (except Newsprint) Mills		750
322122	Newsprint Mills		750
322130	Paperboard Mills		750
322211	Corrugated and Solid Fiber Box Manufacturing		500
322212	Folding Paperboard Box Manufacturing		750
322219	Other Paperboard Container Manufacturing		750
322220	Paper Bag and Coated and Treated Paper Manufacturing		500
322230	Stationery Product Manufacturing		500
322291	Sanitary Paper Product Manufacturing		500
322299	All Other Converted Paper Product Manufacturing		500
Subsector 323 – Printing and Related Support Activities			
323111	Commercial Printing (except Screen and Books)		500
323113	Commercial Screen Printing		500
323117	Books Printing		500
323120	Support Activities for Printing		500
Subsector 324 – Petroleum and Coal Products Manufacturing			
324110	Petroleum Refineries[4]		1,500[4]
324121	Asphalt Paving Mixture and Block Manufacturing		500
324122	Asphalt Shingle and Coating Materials Manufacturing		750
324191	Petroleum Lubricating Oil and Grease Manufacturing		500
324199	All Other Petroleum and Coal Products Manufacturing		500
Subsector 325 – Chemical Manufacturing			
325110	Petrochemical Manufacturing		1,000
325120	Industrial Gas Manufacturing		1,000
325130	Synthetic Dye and Pigment Manufacturing		1,000
325180	Other Basic Inorganic Chemical Manufacturing		1,000
325193	Ethyl Alcohol Manufacturing		1,000
325194	Cyclic Crude, Intermediate, and Gum and Wood Chemical Manufacturing		750
325199	All Other Basic Organic Chemical Manufacturing		1,000

NAICS Codes	NAICS Industry Description	Size Standards in millions of dollars	Size standards in number of employees
325211	Plastics Material and Resin Manufacturing		750
325212	Synthetic Rubber Manufacturing		1,000
325220	Artificial and Synthetic Fibers and Filaments Manufacturing		1,000
325311	Nitrogenous Fertilizer Manufacturing		1,000
325312	Phosphatic Fertilizer Manufacturing		500
325314	Fertilizer (Mixing Only) Manufacturing		500
325320	Pesticide and Other Agricultural Chemical Manufacturing		500
325411	Medicinal and Botanical Manufacturing		750
325412	Pharmaceutical Preparation Manufacturing		750
325413	In-Vitro Diagnostic Substance Manufacturing		500
325414	Biological Product (except Diagnostic) Manufacturing		500
325510	Paint and Coating Manufacturing		500
325520	Adhesive Manufacturing		500
325611	Soap and Other Detergent Manufacturing		750
325612	Polish and Other Sanitation Good Manufacturing		500
325613	Surface Active Agent Manufacturing		500
325620	Toilet Preparation Manufacturing		500
325910	Printing Ink Manufacturing		500
325920	Explosives Manufacturing		750
325991	Custom Compounding of Purchased Resins		500
325992	Photographic Film, Paper, Plate and Chemical Manufacturing		500
325998	All Other Miscellaneous Chemical Product and Preparation Manufacturing		500
Subsector 326 – Plastics and Rubber Products Manufacturing			
326111	Plastic Bag and Pouch Manufacturing		500
326112	Plastics Packaging Film and Sheet (including Laminated) Manufacturing		500
326113	Unlaminated Plastics Film and Sheet (except Packaging) Manufacturing		500
326121	Unlaminated Plastics Profile Shape Manufacturing		500
326122	Plastics Pipe and Pipe Fitting Manufacturing		500
326130	Laminated Plastics Plate, Sheet (except Packaging), and Shape Manufacturing		500
326140	Polystyrene Foam Product Manufacturing		500

NAICS Codes	NAICS Industry Description	Size Standards in millions of dollars	Size standards in number of employees
326150	Urethane and Other Foam Product (except Polystyrene) Manufacturing		500
326160	Plastics Bottle Manufacturing		500
326191	Plastics Plumbing Fixture Manufacturing		500
326199	All Other Plastics Product Manufacturing		750
326211	Tire Manufacturing (except Retreading)[5]		1,000[5]
326212	Tire Retreading		500
326220	Rubber and Plastics Hoses and Belting Manufacturing		500
326291	Rubber Product Manufacturing for Mechanical Use		500
326299	All Other Rubber Product Manufacturing		500
Subsector 327 – Nonmetallic Mineral Product Manufacturing			
327110	Pottery, Ceramics, and Plumbing Fixture Manufacturing		750
327120	Clay Building Material and Refractories Manufacturing		750
327211	Flat Glass Manufacturing		1,000
327212	Other Pressed and Blown Glass and Glassware Manufacturing		750
327213	Glass Container Manufacturing		750
327215	Glass Product Manufacturing Made of Purchased Glass		500
327310	Cement Manufacturing		750
327320	Ready-Mix Concrete Manufacturing		500
327331	Concrete Block and Brick Manufacturing		500
327332	Concrete Pipe Manufacturing		500
327390	Other Concrete Product Manufacturing		500
327410	Lime Manufacturing		500
327420	Gypsum Product Manufacturing		1,000
327910	Abrasive Product Manufacturing		500
327991	Cut Stone and Stone Product Manufacturing		500
327992	Ground or Treated Mineral and Earth Manufacturing		500
327993	Mineral Wool Manufacturing		750
327999	All Other Miscellaneous Nonmetallic Mineral Product Manufacturing		500

NAICS Codes	NAICS Industry Description	Size Standards in millions of dollars	Size standards in number of employees
Subsector 331 – Primary Metal Manufacturing			
331110	Iron and Steel Mills and Ferroalloy Manufacturing		1,000
331210	Iron and Steel Pipe and Tube Manufacturing from Purchased Steel		1,000
331221	Rolled Steel Shape Manufacturing		1,000
331222	Steel Wire Drawing		1,000
331313	Alumina Refining and Primary Aluminum Production		1,000
331314	Secondary Smelting and Alloying of Aluminum		750
331315	Aluminum Sheet, Plate and Foil Manufacturing		750
331318	Other Aluminum Rolling, Drawing, and Extruding		750
331410	Nonferrous Metal (except Aluminum) Smelting and Refining		1,000
331420	Copper Rolling, Drawing, Extruding, and Alloying		1,000
331491	Nonferrous Metal (except Copper and Aluminum) Rolling, Drawing and Extruding		750
331492	Secondary Smelting, Refining, and Alloying of Nonferrous Metal (except Copper and Aluminum)		750
331511	Iron Foundries		500
331512	Steel Investment Foundries		500
331513	Steel Foundries (except Investment)		500
331523	Nonferrous Metal Die-Casting Foundries		500
331524	Aluminum Foundries (except Die-Casting)		500
331529	Other Nonferrous Metal Foundries (except Die-Casting)		500
Subsector 332 – Fabricated Metal Product Manufacturing			
332111	Iron and Steel Forging		500
332112	Nonferrous Forging		500
332114	Custom Roll Forming		500
332117	Powder Metallurgy Part Manufacturing		500
332119	Metal Crown, Closure, and Other Metal Stamping (except Automotive)		500
332215	Metal Kitchen Cookware, Utensil, Cutlery, and Flatware (except Precious) Manufacturing		500
332216	Saw Blade and Handtool Manufacturing		500
332311	Prefabricated Metal Building and Component Manufacturing		500
332312	Fabricated Structural Metal Manufacturing		500

NAICS Codes	NAICS Industry Description	Size Standards in millions of dollars	Size standards in number of employees
332313	Plate Work Manufacturing		500
332321	Metal Window and Door Manufacturing		500
332322	Sheet Metal Work Manufacturing		500
332323	Ornamental and Architectural Metal Work Manufacturing		500
332410	Power Boiler and Heat Exchanger Manufacturing		500
332420	Metal Tank (Heavy Gauge) Manufacturing		500
332431	Metal Can Manufacturing		1,000
332439	Other Metal Container Manufacturing		500
332510	Hardware Manufacturing		500
332613	Spring Manufacturing		500
332618	Other Fabricated Wire Product Manufacturing		500
332710	Machine Shops		500
332721	Precision Turned Product Manufacturing		500
332722	Bolt, Nut, Screw, Rivet and Washer Manufacturing		500
332811	Metal Heat Treating		750
332812	Metal Coating, Engraving (except Jewelry and Silverware), and Allied Services to Manufacturers		500
332813	Electroplating, Plating, Polishing, Anodizing and Coloring		500
332911	Industrial Valve Manufacturing		500
332912	Fluid Power Valve and Hose Fitting Manufacturing		500
332913	Plumbing Fixture Fitting and Trim Manufacturing		500
332919	Other Metal Valve and Pipe Fitting Manufacturing		500
332991	Ball and Roller Bearing Manufacturing		750
332992	Small Arms Ammunition Manufacturing		1,000
332993	Ammunition (except Small Arms) Manufacturing		1,500
332994	Small Arms, Ordnance, and Ordnance Accessories Manufacturing		1,000
332996	Fabricated Pipe and Pipe Fitting Manufacturing		500
332999	All Other Miscellaneous Fabricated Metal Product Manufacturing		750
Subsector 333 – Machinery Manufacturing[6]			
333111	Farm Machinery and Equipment Manufacturing		500
333112	Lawn and Garden Tractor and Home Lawn and Garden Equipment Manufacturing		500
333120	Construction Machinery Manufacturing		750

NAICS Codes	NAICS Industry Description	Size Standards in millions of dollars	Size standards in number of employees
333131	Mining Machinery and Equipment Manufacturing		500
333132	Oil and Gas Field Machinery and Equipment Manufacturing		500
333241	Food Product Machinery Manufacturing		500
333242	Semiconductor Machinery Manufacturing		500
333243	Sawmill, Woodworking, and Paper Machinery Manufacturing		500
333244	Printing Machinery and Equipment Manufacturing		500
333249	Other Industrial Machinery Manufacturing		500
333314	Optical Instrument and Lens Manufacturing		500
333316	Photographic and Photocopying Equipment Manufacturing		1,000
333318	Other Commercial and Service Industry Machinery Manufacturing		1,000
333413	Industrial and Commercial Fan and Blower and Air Purification Equipment Manufacturing		500
333414	Heating Equipment (except Warm Air Furnaces) Manufacturing		500
333415	Air-Conditioning and Warm Air Heating Equipment and Commercial and Industrial Refrigeration Equipment Manufacturing		750
333511	Industrial Mold Manufacturing		500
333514	Special Die and Tool, Die Set, Jig and Fixture Manufacturing		500
333515	Cutting Tool and Machine Tool Accessory Manufacturing		500
333517	Machine Tool Manufacturing		500
333519	Rolling Mill and Other Metalworking Machinery Manufacturing		500
333611	Turbine and Turbine Generator Set Unit Manufacturing		1,000
333612	Speed Changer, Industrial High-Speed Drive and Gear Manufacturing		500
333613	Mechanical Power Transmission Equipment Manufacturing		500
333618	Other Engine Equipment Manufacturing		1,000
333911	Pump and Pumping Equipment Manufacturing		500

NAICS Codes	NAICS Industry Description	Size Standards in millions of dollars	Size standards in number of employees
333912	Air and Gas Compressor Manufacturing		500
333913	Measuring and Dispensing Pump Manufacturing		500
333921	Elevator and Moving Stairway Manufacturing		500
333922	Conveyor and Conveying Equipment Manufacturing		500
333923	Overhead Traveling Crane, Hoist and Monorail System Manufacturing		500
333924	Industrial Truck, Tractor, Trailer and Stacker Machinery Manufacturing		750
333991	Power-Driven Hand Tool Manufacturing		500
333992	Welding and Soldering Equipment Manufacturing		500
333993	Packaging Machinery Manufacturing		500
333994	Industrial Process Furnace and Oven Manufacturing		500
333995	Fluid Power Cylinder and Actuator Manufacturing		500
333996	Fluid Power Pump and Motor Manufacturing		500
333997	Scale and Balance Manufacturing		500
333999	All Other Miscellaneous General Purpose Machinery Manufacturing		500
Subsector 334 – Computer and Electronic Product Manufacturing[6]			
334111	Electronic Computer Manufacturing		1,000
334112	Computer Storage Device Manufacturing		1,000
334118	Computer Terminal and Other Computer Peripheral Equipment Manufacturing		1,000
334210	Telephone Apparatus Manufacturing		1,000
334220	Radio and Television Broadcasting and Wireless Communications Equipment Manufacturing		750
334290	Other Communications Equipment Manufacturing		750
334310	Audio and Video Equipment Manufacturing		750
334412	Bare Printed Circuit Board Manufacturing		500
334413	Semiconductor and Related Device Manufacturing		500
334416	Capacitor, Resistor, Coil, Transformer, and Other Inductor Manufacturing		500
334417	Electronic Connector Manufacturing		500
334418	Printed Circuit Assembly (Electronic Assembly) Manufacturing		500
334419	Other Electronic Component Manufacturing		500
334510	Electromedical and Electrotherapeutic Apparatus Manufacturing		500

NAICS Codes	NAICS Industry Description	Size Standards in millions of dollars	Size standards in number of employees
334511	Search, Detection, Navigation, Guidance, Aeronautical, and Nautical System and Instrument Manufacturing		750
334512	Automatic Environmental Control Manufacturing for Residential, Commercial and Appliance Use		500
334513	Instruments and Related Products Manufacturing for Measuring, Displaying, and Controlling Industrial Process Variables		500
334514	Totalizing Fluid Meter and Counting Device Manufacturing		500
334515	Instrument Manufacturing for Measuring and Testing Electricity and Electrical Signals		500
334516	Analytical Laboratory Instrument Manufacturing		500
334517	Irradiation Apparatus Manufacturing		500
334519	Other Measuring and Controlling Device Manufacturing		500
334613	Blank Magnetic and Optical Recording Media Manufacturing		1,000
334614	Software and Other Prerecorded Compact Disc, Tape, and Record Reproducing		750
Subsector 335 – Electrical Equipment, Appliance and Component Manufacturing[6]			
335110	Electric Lamp Bulb and Part Manufacturing		1,000
335121	Residential Electric Lighting Fixture Manufacturing		500
335122	Commercial, Industrial and Institutional Electric Lighting Fixture Manufacturing		500
335129	Other Lighting Equipment Manufacturing		500
335210	Small Electrical Appliance Manufacturing		750
335221	Household Cooking Appliance Manufacturing		750
335222	Household Refrigerator and Home Freezer Manufacturing		1,000
335224	Household Laundry Equipment Manufacturing		1,000
335228	Other Major Household Appliance Manufacturing		500
335311	Power, Distribution and Specialty Transformer Manufacturing		750
335312	Motor and Generator Manufacturing		1,000
335313	Switchgear and Switchboard Apparatus Manufacturing		750

NAICS Codes	NAICS Industry Description	Size Standards in millions of dollars	Size standards in number of employees
335314	Relay and Industrial Control Manufacturing		750
335911	Storage Battery Manufacturing		500
335912	Primary Battery Manufacturing		1,000
335921	Fiber Optic Cable Manufacturing		1,000
335929	Other Communication and Energy Wire Manufacturing		1,000
335931	Current-Carrying Wiring Device Manufacturing		500
335932	Noncurrent-Carrying Wiring Device Manufacturing		500
335991	Carbon and Graphite Product Manufacturing		750
335999	All Other Miscellaneous Electrical Equipment and Component Manufacturing		500
Subsector 336 – Transportation Equipment Manufacturing[6]			
336111	Automobile Manufacturing		1,000
336112	Light Truck and Utility Vehicle Manufacturing		1,000
336120	Heavy Duty Truck Manufacturing		1,000
336211	Motor Vehicle Body Manufacturing		1,000
336212	Truck Trailer Manufacturing		500
336213	Motor Home Manufacturing		1,000
336214	Travel Trailer and Camper Manufacturing		500
336310	Motor Vehicle Gasoline Engine and Engine Parts Manufacturing		750
336320	Motor Vehicle Electrical and Electronic Equipment Manufacturing		750
336330	Motor Vehicle Steering and Suspension Components (except Spring) Manufacturing		750
336340	Motor Vehicle Brake System Manufacturing		750
336350	Motor Vehicle Transmission and Power Train Parts Manufacturing		750
336360	Motor Vehicle Seating and Interior Trim Manufacturing		500
336370	Motor Vehicle Metal Stamping		500
336390	Other Motor Vehicle Parts Manufacturing		750
336411	Aircraft Manufacturing		1,500
336412	Aircraft Engine and Engine Parts Manufacturing		1,000
336413	Other Aircraft Part and Auxiliary Equipment Manufacturing[7]		1,000[7]
336414	Guided Missile and Space Vehicle Manufacturing		1,000

NAICS Codes	NAICS Industry Description	Size Standards in millions of dollars	Size standards in number of employees
336415	Guided Missile and Space Vehicle Propulsion Unit and Propulsion Unit Parts Manufacturing		1,000
336419	Other Guided Missile and Space Vehicle Parts and Auxiliary Equipment Manufacturing		1,000
336510	Railroad Rolling Stock Manufacturing		1,000
336611	Ship Building and Repairing		1,000
336612	Boat Building		500
336991	Motorcycle, Bicycle and Parts Manufacturing		500
336992	Military Armored Vehicle, Tank and Tank Component Manufacturing		1,000
336999	All Other Transportation Equipment Manufacturing		500
Subsector 337 – Furniture and Related Product Manufacturing			
337110	Wood Kitchen Cabinet and Counter Top Manufacturing		500
337121	Upholstered Household Furniture Manufacturing		500
337122	Nonupholstered Wood Household Furniture Manufacturing		500
337124	Metal Household Furniture Manufacturing		500
337125	Household Furniture (except Wood and Metal) Manufacturing		500
337127	Institutional Furniture Manufacturing		500
337211	Wood Office Furniture Manufacturing		500
337212	Custom Architectural Woodwork and Millwork Manufacturing		500
337214	Office Furniture (Except Wood) Manufacturing		500
337215	Showcase, Partition, Shelving, and Locker Manufacturing		500
337910	Mattress Manufacturing		500
337920	Blind and Shade Manufacturing		500
Subsector 339 – Miscellaneous Manufacturing			
339112	Surgical and Medical Instrument Manufacturing		500
339113	Surgical Appliance and Supplies Manufacturing		500
339114	Dental Equipment and Supplies Manufacturing		500
339115	Ophthalmic Goods Manufacturing		500
339116	Dental Laboratories		500
339910	Jewelry and Silverware Manufacturing		500
339920	Sporting and Athletic Goods Manufacturing		500

NAICS Codes	NAICS Industry Description	Size Standards in millions of dollars	Size standards in number of employees
339930	Doll, Toy, and Game Manufacturing		500
339940	Office Supplies (except Paper) Manufacturing		500
339950	Sign Manufacturing		500
339991	Gasket, Packing, and Sealing Device Manufacturing		500
339992	Musical Instrument Manufacturing		500
339993	Fastener, Button, Needle and Pin Manufacturing		500
339994	Broom, Brush and Mop Manufacturing		500
339995	Burial Casket Manufacturing		500
339999	All Other Miscellaneous Manufacturing		500
	**Sector 42 – Wholesale Trade**		

Sector 42 – Wholesale Trade

(These NAICS codes shall not be used to classify Government acquisitions for supplies. They also shall not be used by Federal government contractors when subcontracting for the acquisition for supplies. The applicable manufacturing NAICS code shall be used to classify acquisitions for supplies. A Wholesale Trade or Retail Trade business concern submitting an offer or a quote on a supply acquisition is categorized as a nonmanufacturer and deemed small if it has 500 or fewer employees and meets the requirements of 13 CFR 121.406.)

Subsector 423 – Merchant Wholesalers, Durable Goods

NAICS Codes	NAICS Industry Description	Size Standards in millions of dollars	Size standards in number of employees
423110	Automobile and Other Motor Vehicle Merchant Wholesalers		100
423120	Motor Vehicle Supplies and New Parts Merchant Wholesalers		100
423130	Tire and Tube Merchant Wholesalers		100
423140	Motor Vehicle Parts (Used) Merchant Wholesalers		100
423210	Furniture Merchant Wholesalers		100
423220	Home Furnishing Merchant Wholesalers		100
423310	Lumber, Plywood, Millwork, and Wood Panel Merchant Wholesalers		100
423320	Brick, Stone, and Related Construction Material Merchant Wholesalers		100
423330	Roofing, Siding, and Insulation Material Merchant Wholesalers		100
423390	Other Construction Material Merchant Wholesalers		100
423410	Photographic Equipment and Supplies Merchant Wholesalers		100
423420	Office Equipment Merchant Wholesalers		100

NAICS Codes	NAICS Industry Description	Size Standards in millions of dollars	Size standards in number of employees
423430	Computer and Computer Peripheral Equipment and Software Merchant Wholesalers		100
423440	Other Commercial Equipment Merchant Wholesalers		100
423450	Medical, Dental, and Hospital Equipment and Supplies Merchant Wholesalers		100
423460	Ophthalmic Goods Merchant Wholesalers		100
423490	Other Professional Equipment and Supplies Merchant Wholesalers		100
423510	Metal Service Centers and Other Metal Merchant Wholesalers		100
423520	Coal and Other Mineral and Ore Merchant Wholesalers		100
423610	Electrical Apparatus and Equipment, Wiring Supplies, and Related Equipment Merchant Wholesalers		100
423620	Household Appliances, Electric Housewares, and Consumer Electronics Merchant Wholesalers		100
423690	Other Electronic Parts and Equipment Merchant Wholesalers		100
423710	Hardware Merchant Wholesalers		100
423720	Plumbing and Heating Equipment and Supplies (Hydronics) Merchant Wholesalers		100
423730	Warm Air Heating and Air-Conditioning Equipment and Supplies Merchant Wholesalers		100
423740	Refrigeration Equipment and Supplies Merchant Wholesalers		100
423810	Construction and Mining (except Oil Well) Machinery and Equipment Merchant Wholesalers		100
423820	Farm and Garden Machinery and Equipment Merchant Wholesalers		100
423830	Industrial Machinery and Equipment Merchant Wholesalers		100
423840	Industrial Supplies Merchant Wholesalers		100
423850	Service Establishment Equipment and Supplies Merchant Wholesalers		100
423860	Transportation Equipment and Supplies (except Motor Vehicle) Merchant Wholesalers		100

NAICS Codes	NAICS Industry Description	Size Standards in millions of dollars	Size standards in number of employees
423910	Sporting and Recreational Goods and Supplies Merchant Wholesalers		100
423920	Toy and Hobby Goods and Supplies Merchant Wholesalers		100
423930	Recyclable Material Merchant Wholesalers		100
423940	Jewelry, Watch, Precious Stone, and Precious Metal Merchant Wholesalers		100
423990	Other Miscellaneous Durable Goods Merchant Wholesalers		100
Subsector 424 – Merchant Wholesalers, Nondurable Goods			
424110	Printing and Writing Paper Merchant Wholesalers		100
424120	Stationary and Office Supplies Merchant Wholesalers		100
424130	Industrial and Personal Service Paper Merchant Wholesalers		100
424210	Drugs and Druggists' Sundries Merchant Wholesalers		100
424310	Piece Goods, Notions, and Other Dry Goods Merchant Wholesalers		100
424320	Men's and Boys' Clothing and Furnishings Merchant Wholesalers		100
424330	Women's, Children's, and Infants' Clothing and Accessories Merchant Wholesalers		100
424340	Footwear Merchant Wholesalers		100
424410	General Line Grocery Merchant Wholesalers		100
424420	Packaged Frozen Food Merchant Wholesalers		100
424430	Dairy Product (except Dried or Canned) Merchant Wholesalers		100
424440	Poultry and Poultry Product Merchant Wholesalers		100
424450	Confectionery Merchant Wholesalers		100
424460	Fish and Seafood Merchant Wholesalers		100
424470	Meat and Meat Product Merchant Wholesalers		100
424480	Fresh Fruit and Vegetable Merchant Wholesalers		100
424490	Other Grocery and Related Products Merchant Wholesalers		100
424510	Grain and Field Bean Merchant Wholesalers		100
424520	Livestock Merchant Wholesalers		100
424590	Other Farm Product Raw Material Merchant Wholesalers		100

NAICS Codes	NAICS Industry Description	Size Standards in millions of dollars	Size standards in number of employees
424610	Plastics Materials and Basic Forms and Shapes Merchant Wholesalers		100
424690	Other Chemical and Allied Products Merchant Wholesalers		100
424710	Petroleum Bulk Stations and Terminals		100
424720	Petroleum and Petroleum Products Merchant Wholesalers (except Bulk Stations and Terminals)		100
424810	Beer and Ale Merchant Wholesalers		100
424820	Wine and Distilled Alcoholic Beverage Merchant Wholesalers		100
424910	Farm Supplies Merchant Wholesalers		100
424920	Book, Periodical, and Newspaper Merchant Wholesalers		100
424930	Flower, Nursery Stock, and Florists' Supplies Merchant Wholesalers		100
424940	Tobacco and Tobacco Product Merchant Wholesalers		100
424950	Paint, Varnish, and Supplies Merchant Wholesalers		100
424990	Other Miscellaneous Nondurable Goods Merchant Wholesalers		100
Subsector 425 – Wholesale Electronic Markets and Agents and Brokers			
425110	Business to Business Electronic Markets		100
425120	Wholesale Trade Agents and Brokers		100
Sector 44 - 45 – Retail Trade			
(These NAICS codes shall not be used to classify Government acquisitions for supplies. They also shall not be used by Federal government contractors when subcontracting for the acquisition for supplies. The applicable manufacturing NAICS code shall be used to classify acquisitions for supplies. A Wholesale Trade or Retail Trade business concern submitting an offer or a quote on a supply acquisition is categorized as a nonmanufacturer and deemed small if it has 500 or fewer employees and meets the requirements of 13 CFR 121.406.)			
Subsector 441 – Motor Vehicle and Parts Dealers			
441110	New Car Dealers		200
441120	Used Car Dealers	$23.0	
441210	Recreational Vehicle Dealers	$30.0	
441222	Boat Dealers	$30.0	
441228	Motorcycle, ATV, and All Other Motor Vehicle Dealers	$30.0	

NAICS Codes	NAICS Industry Description	Size Standards in millions of dollars	Size standards in number of employees
441310	Automotive Parts and Accessories Stores	$14.0	
441320	Tire Dealers	$14.0	
Subsector 442 – Furniture and Home Furnishings Stores			
442110	Furniture Stores	$19.0	
442210	Floor Covering Stores	$7.0	
442291	Window Treatment Stores	$7.0	
442299	All Other Home Furnishings Stores	$19.0	
Subsector 443 – Electronics and Appliance Stores			
443141	Household Appliance Stores	$10.0	
443142	Electronics Stores	$30.0	
Subsector 444 – Building Material and Garden Equipment and Supplies Dealers			
444110	Home Centers	$35.5	
444120	Paint and Wallpaper Stores	$25.5	
444130	Hardware Stores	$7.0	
444190	Other Building Material Dealers	$19.0	
444210	Outdoor Power Equipment Stores	$7.0	
444220	Nursery and Garden Centers	$10.0	
Subsector 445 – Food and Beverage Stores			
445110	Supermarkets and Other Grocery (except Convenience) Stores	$30.0	
445120	Convenience Stores	$27.0	
445210	Meat Markets	$7.0	
445220	Fish and Seafood Markets	$7.0	
445230	Fruit and Vegetable Markets	$7.0	
445291	Baked Goods Stores	$7.0	
445292	Confectionery and Nut Stores	$7.0	
445299	All Other Specialty Food Stores	$7.0	
445310	Beer, Wine and Liquor Stores	$7.0	
Subsector 446 – Health and Personal Care Stores			
446110	Pharmacies and Drug Stores	$25.5	
446120	Cosmetics, Beauty Supplies and Perfume Stores	$25.5	
446130	Optical Goods Stores	$19.0	
446191	Food (Health) Supplement Stores	$14.0	
446199	All Other Health and Personal Care Stores	$7.0	
Subsector 447 – Gasoline Stations			
447110	Gasoline Stations with Convenience Stores	$27.0	
447190	Other Gasoline Stations	$14.0	

NAICS Codes	NAICS Industry Description	Size Standards in millions of dollars	Size standards in number of employees
Subsector 448 – Clothing and Clothing Accessories Stores			
448110	Men's Clothing Stores	$10.0	
448120	Women's Clothing Stores	$25.5	
448130	Children's and Infants' Clothing Stores	$30.0	
448140	Family Clothing Stores	$35.5	
448150	Clothing Accessories Stores	$14.0	
448190	Other Clothing Stores	$19.0	
448210	Shoe Stores	$25.5	
448310	Jewelry Stores	$14.0	
448320	Luggage and Leather Goods Stores	$25.5	
Subsector 451 – Sporting Good, Hobby, Book and Music Stores			
451110	Sporting Goods Stores	$14.0	
451120	Hobby, Toy and Game Stores	$25.5	
451130	Sewing, Needlework and Piece Goods Stores	$25.5	
451140	Musical Instrument and Supplies Stores	$10.0	
451211	Book Stores	$25.5	
451212	News Dealers and Newsstands	$7.0	
Subsector 452 – General Merchandise Stores			
452111	Department Stores (except Discount Department Stores)	$30.0	
452112	Discount Department Stores	$27.0	
452910	Warehouse Clubs and Superstores	$27.0	
452990	All Other General Merchandise Stores	$30.0	
Subsector 453 – Miscellaneous Store Retailers			
453110	Florists	$7.0	
453210	Office Supplies and Stationery Stores	$30.0	
453220	Gift, Novelty and Souvenir Stores	$7.0	
453310	Used Merchandise Stores	$7.0	
453910	Pet and Pet Supplies Stores	$19.0	
453920	Art Dealers	$7.0	
453930	Manufactured (Mobile) Home Dealers	$14.0	
453991	Tobacco Stores	$7.0	
453998	All Other Miscellaneous Store Retailers (except Tobacco Stores)	$7.0	
Subsector 454 – Nonstore Retailers			
454111	Electronic Shopping	$30.0	
454112	Electronic Auctions	$35.5	

NAICS Codes	NAICS Industry Description	Size Standards in millions of dollars	Size standards in number of employees
454113	Mail-Order Houses	$35.5	
454210	Vending Machine Operators	$10.0	
454310	Fuel Dealers		50
454390	Other Direct Selling Establishments	$7.0	
Sector 48 - 49 – Transportation and Warehousing			
Subsector 481 – Air Transportation			
481111	Scheduled Passenger Air Transportation		1,500
481112	Scheduled Freight Air Transportation		1,500
481211	Nonscheduled Chartered Passenger Air Transportation		1,500
Except,	Offshore Marine Air Transportation Services	$28.0	
481212	Nonscheduled Chartered Freight Air Transportation		1,500
Except,	Offshore Marine Air Transportation Services	$28.0	
481219	Other Nonscheduled Air Transportation	$14.0	
Subsector 482 – Rail Transportation			
482111	Line-Haul Railroads		1,500
482112	Short Line Railroads		500
Subsector 483 – Water Transportation[15]			
483111	Deep Sea Freight Transportation		500
483112	Deep Sea Passenger Transportation		500
483113	Coastal and Great Lakes Freight Transportation		500
483114	Coastal and Great Lakes Passenger Transportation		500
483211	Inland Water Freight Transportation		500
483212	Inland Water Passenger Transportation		500
Subsector 484 – Truck Transportation			
484110	General Freight Trucking, Local	$25.5	
484121	General Freight Trucking, Long-Distance, Truckload	$25.5	
484122	General Freight Trucking, Long-Distance, Less Than Truckload	$25.5	
484210	Used Household and Office Goods Moving	$25.5	
484220	Specialized Freight (except Used Goods) Trucking, Local	$25.5	
484230	Specialized Freight (except Used Goods) Trucking, Long-Distance	$25.5	
Subsector 485 – Transit and Ground Passenger Transportation			
485111	Mixed Mode Transit Systems	$14.0	
485112	Commuter Rail Systems	$14.0	

NAICS Codes	NAICS Industry Description	Size Standards in millions of dollars	Size standards in number of employees
485113	Bus and Other Motor Vehicle Transit Systems	$14.0	
485119	Other Urban Transit Systems	$14.0	
485210	Interurban and Rural Bus Transportation	$14.0	
485310	Taxi Service	$14.0	
485320	Limousine Service	$14.0	
485410	School and Employee Bus Transportation	$14.0	
485510	Charter Bus Industry	$14.0	
485991	Special Needs Transportation	$14.0	
485999	All Other Transit and Ground Passenger Transportation	$14.0	
Subsector 486 – Pipeline Transportation			
486110	Pipeline Transportation of Crude Oil		1,500
486210	Pipeline Transportation of Natural Gas	$25.5	
486910	Pipeline Transportation of Refined Petroleum Products		1,500
486990	All Other Pipeline Transportation	$34.5	
Subsector 487 – Scenic and Sightseeing Transportation			
487110	Scenic and Sightseeing Transportation, Land	$7.0	
487210	Scenic and Sightseeing Transportation, Water	$7.0	
487990	Scenic and Sightseeing Transportation, Other	$7.0	
Subsector 488 – Support Activities for Transportation			
488111	Air Traffic Control	$30.0	
488119	Other Airport Operations	$30.0	
488190	Other Support Activities for Air Transportation	$30.0	
488210	Support Activities for Rail Transportation	$14.0	
488310	Port and Harbor Operations	$35.5	
488320	Marine Cargo Handling	$35.5	
488330	Navigational Services to Shipping	$35.5	
488390	Other Support Activities for Water Transportation	$35.5	
488410	Motor Vehicle Towing	$7.0	
488490	Other Support Activities for Road Transportation	$7.0	
488510	Freight Transportation Arrangement[10]	$14.0[10]	
Except,	Non-Vessel Owning Common Carriers and Household Goods Forwarders	$25.5	
488991	Packing and Crating	$25.5	
488999	All Other Support Activities for Transportation	$7.0	

NAICS Codes	NAICS Industry Description	Size Standards in millions of dollars	Size standards in number of employees
Subsector 491 – Postal Service			
491110	Postal Service	$7.0	
Subsector 492 – Couriers and Messengers			
492110	Couriers and Express Delivery Services		1,500
492210	Local Messengers and Local Delivery	$25.5	
Subsector 493 – Warehousing and Storage			
493110	General Warehousing and Storage	$25.5	
493120	Refrigerated Warehousing and Storage	$25.5	
493130	Farm Product Warehousing and Storage	$25.5	
493190	Other Warehousing and Storage	$25.5	
Sector 51 – Information			
Subsector 511 – Publishing Industries (except Internet)			
511110	Newspaper Publishers		500
511120	Periodical Publishers		500
511130	Book Publishers		500
511140	Directory and Mailing List Publishers		500
511191	Greeting Card Publishers		500
511199	All Other Publishers		500
511210	Software Publishers	$35.5	
Subsector 512 – Motion Picture and Sound Recording Industries			
512110	Motion Picture and Video Production	$30.0	
512120	Motion Picture and Video Distribution	$29.5	
512131	Motion Picture Theaters (except Drive-Ins)	$35.5	
512132	Drive-In Motion Picture Theaters	$7.0	
512191	Teleproduction and Other Postproduction Services	$29.5	
512199	Other Motion Picture and Video Industries	$19.0	
512210	Record Production	$7.0	
512220	Integrated Record Production/Distribution		750
512230	Music Publishers		500
512240	Sound Recording Studios	$7.0	
512290	Other Sound Recording Industries	$10.0	
Subsector 515 – Broadcasting (except Internet)			
515111	Radio Networks	$30.0	
515112	Radio Stations	$35.5	
515120	Television Broadcasting	$35.5	
515210	Cable and Other Subscription Programming	$35.5	

NAICS Codes	NAICS Industry Description	Size Standards in millions of dollars	Size standards in number of employees
Subsector 517 – Telecommunications			
517110	Wired Telecommunications Carriers		1,500
517210	Wireless Telecommunications Carriers (except Satellite)		1,500
517410	Satellite Telecommunications	$30.0	
517911	Telecommunications Resellers		1,500
517919	All Other Telecommunications	$30.0	
Subsector 518 –Data Processing, Hosting, and Related Services			
518210	Data Processing, Hosting, and Related Services	$30.0	
Subsector 519 – Other Information Services			
519110	News Syndicates	$25.5	
519120	Libraries and Archives	$14.0	
519130	Internet Publishing and Broadcasting and Web Search Portals		500
519190	All Other Information Services	$25.5	
Sector 52 – Finance and Insurance			
Subsector 522 – Credit Intermediation and Related Activities			
522110	Commercial Banking[8]	$175 million in assets[8]	
522120	Savings Institutions[8]	$175 million in assets[8]	
522130	Credit Unions[8]	$175 million in assets[8]	
522190	Other Depository Credit Intermediation[8]	$175 million in assets[8]	
522210	Credit Card Issuing[8]	$175 million in assets[8]	
522220	Sales Financing	$7.0	
522291	Consumer Lending	$7.0	
522292	Real Estate Credit	$7.0	
522293	International Trade Financing[8]	$175 million in assets[8]	

NAICS Codes	NAICS Industry Description	Size Standards in millions of dollars	Size standards in number of employees
522294	Secondary Market Financing	$7.0	
522298	All Other Nondepository Credit Intermediation	$7.0	
522310	Mortgage and Nonmortgage Loan Brokers	$7.0	
522320	Financial Transactions, Reserve, and Clearinghouse Activities	$7.0	
522390	Other Activities Related to Credit Intermediation	$7.0	
Subsector 523 – Financial Investments and Related Activities			
523110	Investment Banking and Securities Dealing	$7.0	
523120	Securities Brokerage	$7.0	
523130	Commodity Contracts Dealing	$7.0	
523140	Commodity Contracts Brokerage	$7.0	
523210	Securities and Commodity Exchanges	$7.0	
523910	Miscellaneous Intermediation	$7.0	
523920	Portfolio Management	$7.0	
523930	Investment Advice	$7.0	
523991	Trust, Fiduciary and Custody Activities	$7.0	
523999	Miscellaneous Financial Investment Activities	$7.0	
Subsector 524 – Insurance Carriers and Related Activities			
524113	Direct Life Insurance Carriers	$7.0	
524114	Direct Health and Medical Insurance Carriers	$7.0	
524126	Direct Property and Casualty Insurance Carriers		1,500
524127	Direct Title Insurance Carriers	$7.0	
524128	Other Direct Insurance (except Life, Health and Medical) Carriers	$7.0	
524130	Reinsurance Carriers	$7.0	
524210	Insurance Agencies and Brokerages	$7.0	
524291	Claims Adjusting	$7.0	
524292	Third Party Administration of Insurance and Pension Funds	$7.0	
524298	All Other Insurance Related Activities	$7.0	
Subsector 525 – Funds, Trusts and Other Financial Vehicles			
525110	Pension Funds	$7.0	
525120	Health and Welfare Funds	$7.0	
525190	Other Insurance Funds	$7.0	
525910	Open-End Investment Funds	$7.0	
525920	Trusts, Estates, and Agency Accounts	$7.0	
525990	Other Financial Vehicles	$7.0	

NAICS Codes	NAICS Industry Description	Size Standards in millions of dollars	Size standards in number of employees
	Sector 53 – Real Estate and Rental and Leasing		
Subsector 531 – Real Estate			
531110	Lessors of Residential Buildings and Dwellings	$25.0	
531120	Lessors of Nonresidential Buildings (except Miniwarehouses)	$25.5	
531130	Lessors of Miniwarehouses and Self Storage Units	$25.5	
531190	Lessors of Other Real Estate Property	$25.5	
Except,	Leasing of Building Space to Federal Government by Owners[9]	$35.5[9]	
531210	Offices of Real Estate Agents and Brokers[10]	$7.0[10]	
531311	Residential Property Managers	$7.0	
531312	Nonresidential Property Managers	$7.0	
531320	Offices of Real Estate Appraisers	$7.0	
531390	Other Activities Related to Real Estate	$7.0	
Subsector 532 – Rental and Leasing Services			
532111	Passenger Car Rental	$35.5	
532112	Passenger Car Leasing	$35.5	
532120	Truck, Utility Trailer, and RV (Recreational Vehicle) Rental and Leasing	$35.5	
532210	Consumer Electronics and Appliances Rental	$35.5	
532220	Formal Wear and Costume Rental	$19.0	
532230	Video Tape and Disc Rental	$25.5	
532291	Home Health Equipment Rental	$30.0	
532292	Recreational Goods Rental	$7.0	
532299	All Other Consumer Goods Rental	$7.0	
532310	General Rental Centers	$7.0	
532411	Commercial Air, Rail, and Water Transportation Equipment Rental and Leasing	$30.0	
532412	Construction, Mining and Forestry Machinery and Equipment Rental and Leasing	$30.0	
532420	Office Machinery and Equipment Rental and Leasing	$30.0	
532490	Other Commercial and Industrial Machinery and Equipment Rental and Leasing	$30.0	
Subsector 533 – Lessors of Nonfinancial Intangible Assets (except Copyrighted Works)			
533110	Lessors of Nonfinancial Intangible Assets (except Copyrighted Works)	$35.5	

NAICS Codes	NAICS Industry Description	Size Standards in millions of dollars	Size standards in number of employees
	**Sector 54 – Professional, Scientific and Technical Services**		
	**Subsector 541 – Professional, Scientific and Technical Services**		
541110	Offices of Lawyers	$10.0	
541191	Title Abstract and Settlement Offices	$10.0	
541199	All Other Legal Services	$10.0	
541211	Offices of Certified Public Accountants	$19.0	
541213	Tax Preparation Services	$19.0	
541214	Payroll Services	$19.0	
541219	Other Accounting Services	$19.0	
541310	Architectural Services	$7.0	
541320	Landscape Architectural Services	$7.0	
541330	Engineering Services	$14.0	
Except,	Military and Aerospace Equipment and Military Weapons	$35.5	
Except,	Contracts and Subcontracts for Engineering Services Awarded Under the National Energy Policy Act of 1992	$35.5	
Except,	Marine Engineering and Naval Architecture	$35.5	
541340	Drafting Services	$7.0	
541350	Building Inspection Services	$7.0	
541360	Geophysical Surveying and Mapping Services	$14.0	
541370	Surveying and Mapping (except Geophysical) Services	$14.0	
541380	Testing Laboratories	$14.0	
541410	Interior Design Services	$7.0	
541420	Industrial Design Services	$7.0	
541430	Graphic Design Services	$7.0	
541490	Other Specialized Design Services	$7.0	
541511	Custom Computer Programming Services	$25.5	
541512	Computer Systems Design Services	$25.5	
541513	Computer Facilities Management Services	$25.5	
541519	Other Computer Related Services	$25.5	
Except,	Information Technology Value Added Resellers[18]		150[18]
541611	Administrative Management and General Management Consulting Services	$14.0	
541612	Human Resources Consulting Services	$14.0	
541613	Marketing Consulting Services	$14.0	

NAICS Codes	NAICS Industry Description	Size Standards in millions of dollars	Size standards in number of employees
541614	Process, Physical Distribution and Logistics Consulting Services	$14.0	
541618	Other Management Consulting Services	$14.0	
541620	Environmental Consulting Services	$14.0	
541690	Other Scientific and Technical Consulting Services	$14.0	
541711	Research and Development in Biotechnology[11]		500[11]
541712	Research and Development in the Physical, Engineering, and Life Sciences (except Biotechnology) [11]		500[11]
Except,	Aircraft		1,500
Except,	Aircraft Parts, and Auxiliary Equipment, and Aircraft Engine Parts		1,000
Except,	Space Vehicles and Guided Missiles, their Propulsion Units, their Propulsion Units Parts, and their Auxiliary Equipment and Parts		1,000
541720	Research and Development in the Social Sciences and Humanities	$19.0	
541810	Advertising Agencies[10]	$14.0[10]	
541820	Public Relations Agencies	$14.0	
541830	Media Buying Agencies	$14.0	
541840	Media Representatives	$14.0	
541850	Outdoor Advertising	$14.0	
541860	Direct Mail Advertising	$14.0	
541870	Advertising Material Distribution Services	$14.0	
541890	Other Services Related to Advertising	$14.0	
541910	Marketing Research and Public Opinion Polling	$14.0	
541921	Photography Studios, Portrait	$7.0	
541922	Commercial Photography	$7.0	
541930	Translation and Interpretation Services	$7.0	
541940	Veterinary Services	$7.0	
541990	All Other Professional, Scientific and Technical Services	$14.0	
Sector 55 – Management of Companies and Enterprises			
Subsector 551 – Management of Companies and Enterprises			
551111	Offices of Bank Holding Companies	$7.0	
551112	Offices of Other Holding Companies	$7.0	

NAICS Codes	NAICS Industry Description	Size Standards in millions of dollars	Size standards in number of employees
Sector 56 – Administrative and Support, Waste Management and Remediation Services			
Subsector 561 – Administrative and Support Services			
561110	Office Administrative Services	$7.0	
561210	Facilities Support Services[12]	$35.5[12]	
561311	Employment Placement Agencies	$25.5	
561312	Executive Search Services	$25.5	
561320	Temporary Help Services	$25.5	
561330	Professional Employer Organizations	$25.5	
561410	Document Preparation Services	$14.0	
561421	Telephone Answering Services	$14.0	
561422	Telemarketing Bureaus and Other contact Centers	$14.0	
561431	Private Mail Centers	$14.0	
561439	Other Business Service Centers (including Copy Shops)	$14.0	
561440	Collection Agencies	$14.0	
561450	Credit Bureaus	$14.0	
561491	Repossession Services	$14.0	
561492	Court Reporting and Stenotype Services	$14.0	
561499	All Other Business Support Services	$14.0	
561510	Travel Agencies[10]	$19.0[10]	
561520	Tour Operators[10]	$19.0[10]	
561591	Convention and Visitors Bureaus	19.0	
561599	All Other Travel Arrangement and Reservation Services	$19.0	
561611	Investigation Services	$19.0	
561612	Security Guards and Patrol Services	$19.0	
561613	Armored Car Services	$19.0	
561621	Security Systems Services (except Locksmiths)	$19.0	
561622	Locksmiths	$19.0	
561710	Exterminating and Pest Control Services	$10.0	
561720	Janitorial Services	$16.5	
561730	Landscaping Services	$7.0	
561740	Carpet and Upholstery Cleaning Services	$5.0	
561790	Other Services to Buildings and Dwellings	$7.0	
561910	Packaging and Labeling Services	$10.0	
561920	Convention and Trade Show Organizers[10]	$10.0[10]	
561990	All Other Support Services	$10.0	

NAICS Codes	NAICS Industry Description	Size Standards in millions of dollars	Size standards in number of employees
Subsector 562 – Waste Management and Remediation Services			
562111	Solid Waste Collection	$35.5	
562112	Hazardous Waste Collection	$35.5	
562119	Other Waste Collection	$35.5	
562211	Hazardous Waste Treatment and Disposal	$35.5	
562212	Solid Waste Landfill	$35.5	
562213	Solid Waste Combustors and Incinerators	$35.5	
562219	Other Nonhazardous Waste Treatment and Disposal	$35.5	
562910	Remediation Services	$19.0	
Except,	Environmental Remediation Services[14]		500[14]
562920	Materials Recovery Facilities	$19.0	
562991	Septic Tank and Related Services	$7.0	
562998	All Other Miscellaneous Waste Management Services	$7.0	
Sector 61 – Educational Services			
Subsector 611 – Educational Services			
611110	Elementary and Secondary Schools	$10.0	
611210	Junior Colleges	$19.0	
611310	Colleges, Universities and Professional Schools	$25.5	
611410	Business and Secretarial Schools	$7.0	
611420	Computer Training	$10.0	
611430	Professional and Management Development Training	$10.0	
611511	Cosmetology and Barber Schools	$7.0	
611512	Flight Training	$25.5	
611513	Apprenticeship Training	$7.0	
611519	Other Technical and Trade Schools	$14.0	
Except,	Job Corps Centers[16]	$35.5[16]	
611610	Fine Arts Schools	$7.0	
611620	Sports and Recreation Instruction	$7.0	
611630	Language Schools	$10.0	
611691	Exam Preparation and Tutoring	$7.0	
611692	Automobile Driving Schools	$7.0	
611699	All Other Miscellaneous Schools and Instruction	$10.0	
611710	Educational Support Services	$14.0	

NAICS Codes	NAICS Industry Description	Size Standards in millions of dollars	Size standards in number of employees
Sector 62 – Health Care and Social Assistance			
Subsector 621 – Ambulatory Health Care Services			
621111	Offices of Physicians (except Mental Health Specialists)	$10.0	
621112	Offices of Physicians, Mental Health Specialists	$10.0	
621210	Offices of Dentists	$7.0	
621310	Offices of Chiropractors	$7.0	
621320	Offices of Optometrists	$7.0	
621330	Offices of Mental Health Practitioners (except Physicians)	$7.0	
621340	Offices of Physical, Occupational and Speech Therapists and Audiologists	$7.0	
621391	Offices of Podiatrists	$7.0	
621399	Offices of All Other Miscellaneous Health Practitioners	$7.0	
621410	Family Planning Centers	$10.0	
621420	Outpatient Mental Health and Substance Abuse Centers	$14.0	
621491	HMO Medical Centers	$30.0	
621492	Kidney Dialysis Centers	$35.5	
621493	Freestanding Ambulatory Surgical and Emergency Centers	$14.0	
621498	All Other Outpatient Care Centers	$19.0	
621511	Medical Laboratories	$30.0	
621512	Diagnostic Imaging Centers	$14.0	
621610	Home Health Care Services	$14.0	
621910	Ambulance Services	$14.0	
621991	Blood and Organ Banks	$30.0	
621999	All Other Miscellaneous Ambulatory Health Care Services	$14.0	
Subsector 622 – Hospitals			
622110	General Medical and Surgical Hospitals	$35.5	
622210	Psychiatric and Substance Abuse Hospitals	$35.5	
622310	Specialty (except Psychiatric and Substance Abuse) Hospitals	$35.5	

NAICS Codes	NAICS Industry Description	Size Standards in millions of dollars	Size standards in number of employees
Subsector 623 – Nursing and Residential Care Facilities			
623110	Nursing Care Facilities (Skilled Nursing Facilities)	$25.5	
623210	Residential Intellectual and Developmental Disability Facilities	$14.0	
623220	Residential Mental Health and Substance Abuse Facilities	$14.0	
623311	Continuing Care Retirement Communities	$25.5	
623312	Assisted Living Facilities for the Elderly	$10.0	
623990	Other Residential Care Facilities	$10.0	
Subsector 624 – Social Assistance			
624110	Child and Youth Services	$10.0	
624120	Services for the Elderly and Persons with Disabilities	$10.0	
624190	Other Individual and Family Services	$10.0	
624210	Community Food Services	$10.0	
624221	Temporary Shelters	$10.0	
624229	Other Community Housing Services	$14.0	
624230	Emergency and Other Relief Services	$30.0	
624310	Vocational Rehabilitation Services	$10.0	
624410	Child Day Care Services	$7.0	
Sector 71 – Arts, Entertainment and Recreation			
Subsector 711 – Performing Arts, Spectator Sports and Related Industries			
711110	Theater Companies and Dinner Theaters	$7.0	
711120	Dance Companies	$7.0	
711130	Musical Groups and Artists	$7.0	
711190	Other Performing Arts Companies	$7.0	
711211	Sports Teams and Clubs	$7.0	
711212	Race Tracks	$7.0	
711219	Other Spectator Sports	$7.0	
711310	Promoters of Performing Arts, Sports and Similar Events with Facilities	$7.0	
711320	Promoters of Performing Arts, Sports and Similar Events without Facilities	$7.0	
711410	Agents and Managers for Artists, Athletes, Entertainers and Other Public Figures	$7.0	
711510	Independent Artists, Writers, and Performers	$7.0	

NAICS Codes	NAICS Industry Description	Size Standards in millions of dollars	Size standards in number of employees
Subsector 712 – Museums, Historical Sites and Similar Institutions			
712110	Museums	$7.0	
712120	Historical Sites	$7.0	
712130	Zoos and Botanical Gardens	$7.0	
712190	Nature Parks and Other Similar Institutions	$7.0	
Subsector 713 – Amusement, Gambling and Recreation Industries			
713110	Amusement and Theme Parks	$7.0	
713120	Amusement Arcades	$7.0	
713210	Casinos (except Casino Hotels)	$7.0	
713290	Other Gambling Industries	$7.0	
713910	Golf Courses and Country Clubs	$7.0	
713920	Skiing Facilities	$7.0	
713930	Marinas	$7.0	
713940	Fitness and Recreational Sports Centers	$7.0	
713950	Bowling Centers	$7.0	
713990	All Other Amusement and Recreation Industries	$7.0	
Sector 72 – Accommodation and Food Services			
Subsector 721 – Accommodation			
721110	Hotels (except Casino Hotels) and Motels	$30.0	
721120	Casino Hotels	$30.0	
721191	Bed-and-Breakfast Inns	$7.0	
721199	All Other Traveler Accommodation	$7.0	
721211	RV (Recreational Vehicle) Parks and Campgrounds	$7.0	
721214	Recreational and Vacation Camps (except Campgrounds)	$7.0	
721310	Rooming and Boarding Houses	$7.0	
Subsector 722 – Food Services and Drinking Places			
722310	Food Service Contractors	$35.5	
722320	Caterers	$7.0	
722330	Mobile Food Services	$7.0	
722410	Drinking Places (Alcoholic Beverages)	$7.0	
722511	Full-Service Restaurants	$7.0	
722513	Limited-Service Restaurants	$10.0	
722514	Cafeterias, Grill Buffets, and Buffets	$25.5	
722515	Snack and Nonalcoholic Beverage Bars	$7.0	

NAICS Codes	NAICS Industry Description	Size Standards in millions of dollars	Size standards in number of employees
	**Sector 81 – Other Services**		
	**Subsector 811 – Repair and Maintenance**		
811111	General Automotive Repair	$7.0	
811112	Automotive Exhaust System Repair	$7.0	
811113	Automotive Transmission Repair	$7.0	
811118	Other Automotive Mechanical and Electrical Repair and Maintenance	$7.0	
811121	Automotive Body, Paint and Interior Repair and Maintenance	$7.0	
811122	Automotive Glass Replacement Shops	$10.0	
811191	Automotive Oil Change and Lubrication Shops	$7.0	
811192	Car Washes	$7.0	
811198	All Other Automotive Repair and Maintenance	$7.0	
811211	Consumer Electronics Repair and Maintenance	$7.0	
811212	Computer and Office Machine Repair and Maintenance	$25.5	
811213	Communication Equipment Repair and Maintenance	$10.0	
811219	Other Electronic and Precision Equipment Repair and Maintenance	$19.0	
811310	Commercial and Industrial Machinery and Equipment (except Automotive and Electronic) Repair and Maintenance	$7.0	
811411	Home and Garden Equipment Repair and Maintenance	$7.0	
811412	Appliance Repair and Maintenance	$14.0	
811420	Reupholstery and Furniture Repair	$7.0	
811430	Footwear and Leather Goods Repair	$7.0	
811490	Other Personal and Household Goods Repair and Maintenance	$7.0	
	**Subsector 812 – Personal and Laundry Services**		
812111	Barber Shops	$7.0	
812112	Beauty Salons	$7.0	
812113	Nail Salons	$7.0	
812191	Diet and Weight Reducing Centers	$19.0	
812199	Other Personal Care Services	$7.0	
812210	Funeral Homes and Funeral Services	$7.0	
812220	Cemeteries and Crematories	$19.0	

NAICS Codes	NAICS Industry Description	Size Standards in millions of dollars	Size standards in number of employees
812310	Coin-Operated Laundries and Drycleaners	$7.0	
812320	Drycleaning and Laundry Services (except Coin-Operated)	$5.0	
812331	Linen Supply	$30.0	
812332	Industrial Launderers	$35.5	
812910	Pet Care (except Veterinary) Services	$7.0	
812921	Photofinishing Laboratories (except One-Hour)	$19.0	
812922	One-Hour Photofinishing	$14.0	
812930	Parking Lots and Garages	$35.5	
812990	All Other Personal Services	$7.0	
Subsector 813 – Religious, Grantmaking, Civic, Professional and Similar Organizations			
813110	Religious Organizations	$7.0	
813211	Grantmaking Foundations	$30.0	
813212	Voluntary Health Organizations	$25.5	
813219	Other Grantmaking and Giving Services	$35.5	
813311	Human Rights Organizations	$25.5	
813312	Environment, Conservation and Wildlife Organizations	$14.0	
813319	Other Social Advocacy Organizations	$7.0	
813410	Civic and Social Organizations	$7.0	
813910	**Business Associations**	**$7.0**	
813920	Professional Organizations	$14.0	
813930	Labor Unions and Similar Labor Organizations	$7.0	
813940	Political Organizations	$7.0	
813990	Other Similar Organizations (except Business, Professional, Labor, and Political Organizations)	$7.0	
Sector 92 – Public Administration[19]			
(Small business size standards are not established for this Sector. Establishments in the Public Administration Sector are Federal, state, and local government agencies which administer and oversee government programs and activities that are not performed by private establishments.)			

Footnotes

1.   NAICS codes 221111, 221112, 221113, 221114, 221115, 221116, 221117, 221118, 221121, 221122 – A firm is small if, including its affiliates, it is primarily engaged in the generation, transmission, and/or distribution of electric energy for sale and its total electric output for the preceding fiscal year did not exceed 4 million megawatt hours.

2.   NAICS code 237990 – Dredging: To be considered small for purposes of Government procurement, a firm must perform at least 40 percent of the volume dredged with its own equipment or equipment owned by another small dredging concern.

3.   NAICS code 311421 – For purposes of Government procurement for food canning and preserving, the standard of 500 employees excludes agricultural labor as defined in section 3306(k) of the Internal Revenue Code, 26 U.S.C. 3306(k).

4.   NAICS code 324110 – For purposes of Government procurement, the petroleum refiner must be a concern that has no more than 1,500 employees nor more than 125,000 barrels per calendar day total Operable Atmospheric Crude Oil Distillation capacity. Capacity includes owned or leased facilities as well as facilities under a processing agreement or an arrangement such as an exchange agreement or a throughput. The total product to be delivered under the contract must be at least 90 percent refined by the successful bidder from either crude oil or bona fide feedstocks.

5.   NAICS code 326211 – For Government procurement, a firm is small for bidding on a contract for pneumatic tires within Census Classification codes 30111 and 30112, provided that:

    a) the value of tires within Census Classification codes 30111 and 30112 which it manufactured in the United States during the previous calendar year is more than 50 percent of the value of its total worldwide manufacture,

    b) the value of pneumatic tires within Census Classification codes 30111 and 30112 comprising its total worldwide manufacture during the preceding calendar year was less than 5 percent of the value of all such tires manufactured in the United States during that period, and

    c) the value of the principal product which it manufactured or otherwise produced, or sold worldwide during the preceding calendar year is less than 10 percent of the total value of such products manufactured or otherwise produced or sold in the United States during that period.

6.   NAICS Subsectors 333, 334, 335 and 336 – For rebuilding machinery or equipment on a factory basis, or equivalent, use the NAICS code for a newly manufactured product. Concerns performing major rebuilding or overhaul activities do not necessarily have to meet the criteria for being a "manufacturer" although the activities may be classified under a manufacturing NAICS code. Ordinary repair services or preservation are not considered rebuilding.

7.   NAICS code 336413 – Contracts for the rebuilding or overhaul of aircraft ground support equipment on a contract basis are classified under NAICS code 336413.

8.   NAICS Codes 522110, 522120, 522130, 522190, 522210 and 522293 – A financial institution's assets are determined by averaging the assets reported on its four quarterly financial statements for the preceding year. "Assets" for the purposes of this size standard means the assets defined according to the Federal Financial Institutions Examination Council 034 call report form.

9.   NAICS code 531190 – Leasing of building space to the Federal Government by Owners: For Government procurement, a size standard of $35.5 million in gross receipts applies to the owners of building space leased to the Federal Government. The standard does not apply to an agent.

10.   NAICS codes 488510, 531210, 541810, 561510, 561520 and 561920 – As measured by total revenues, but excluding funds received in trust for an unaffiliated third party, such as bookings or sales subject to commissions. The commissions received are included as revenue.

11.   NAICS code 541711 and 541712 – For research and development contracts requiring the delivery of a manufactured product, the appropriate size standard is that of the manufacturing industry.

    a) "Research and Development" means laboratory or other physical research and development. It does not include economic, educational, engineering, operations, systems, or other nonphysical research; or computer programming, data processing, commercial and/or medical laboratory testing.

    b) For purposes of the Small Business Innovation Research (SBIR) program only, a different definition has been established by law. See section 121.701 of these regulations.

    c) "Research and Development" for guided missiles and space vehicles includes evaluations and simulation, and other services requiring thorough knowledge of complete missiles and spacecraft.

12.   NAICS 561210 – Facilities Support Services:

a) If one or more activities of Facilities Support Services as defined in paragraph (b) (below in this footnote) can be identified with a specific industry and that industry accounts for 50% or more of the value of an entire procurement, then the proper classification of the procurement is that of the specific industry, not Facilities Support Services.

b) "Facilities Support Services" requires the performance of three or more separate activities in the areas of services or specialty trade contractors industries. If services are performed, these service activities must each be in a separate NAICS industry. If the procurement requires the use of specialty trade contractors (plumbing, painting, plastering, carpentry, *etc.*), all such specialty trade contractors activities are considered a single activity and classified as "Building and Property Specialty Trade Services." Since "Building and Property Specialty Trade Services" is only one activity, two additional activities of separate NAICS industries are required for a procurement to be classified as "Facilities Support Services."

13.   NAICS code 238990 – Building and Property Specialty Trade Services: If a procurement requires the use of multiple specialty trade contractors (i.e., plumbing, painting, plastering, carpentry, etc.), and no specialty trade accounts for 50% or more of the value of the procurement, all such specialty trade contractors activities are considered a single activity and classified as Building and Property Specialty Trade Services.

14.   NAICS 562910 – Environmental Remediation Services:

a) For SBA assistance as a small business concern in the industry of Environmental Remediation Services, other than for Government procurement, a concern must be engaged primarily in furnishing a range of services for the remediation of a contaminated environment to an acceptable condition including, but not limited to, preliminary assessment, site inspection, testing, remedial investigation, feasibility studies, remedial design, containment, remedial action, removal of contaminated materials, storage of contaminated materials and security and site closeouts. If one of such activities accounts for 50 percent or more of a concern's total revenues, employees, or other related factors, the concern's primary industry is that of the particular industry and not the Environmental Remediation Services Industry.

b) For purposes of classifying a Government procurement as Environmental Remediation Services, the general purpose of the procurement must be to restore or directly support the restoration of a contaminated environment. This includes activities such as preliminary assessment, site inspection, testing, remedial investigation, feasibility studies, remedial design, remediation services, containment, and removal of contaminated materials or security and site closeouts. The general purpose of the procurement need not necessarily include remedial actions. Also, the procurement must be composed of activities in three or more separate industries with separate

NAICS codes or, in some instances (e.g., engineering), smaller sub-components of NAICS codes with separate and distinct size standards. These activities may include, but are not limited to, separate activities in industries such as: Heavy Construction; Special Trade Contractors; Engineering Services; Architectural Services; Management Consulting Services; Hazardous and Other Waste Collection; Remediation Services; Testing Laboratories; and Research and Development in the Physical, Engineering, and Life Sciences. If any activity in the procurement can be identified with a separate NAICS code, or component of a code with a separate distinct size standard, and that industry accounts for 50 percent or more of the value of the entire procurement, then the proper size standard is the one for that particular industry, and not the Environmental Remediation Service size standard.

15.   Subsector 483 – Water Transportation - Offshore Marine Services: The applicable size standard shall be $28.0 million for firms furnishing specific transportation services to concerns engaged in offshore oil and/or natural gas exploration, drilling production, or marine research; such services encompass passenger and freight transportation, anchor handling, and related logistical services to and from the work site.

16.   NAICS code 611519 – Job Corps Centers. For classifying a Federal procurement, the purpose of the solicitation must be for the management and operation of a U.S. Department of Labor Job Corps Center. The activities involved include admissions activities, life skills training, educational activities, comprehensive career preparation activities, career development activities, career transition activities, as well as the management and support functions and services needed to operate and maintain the facility. For SBA assistance as a small business concern, other than for Federal Government procurements, a concern must be primarily engaged in providing the services to operate and maintain Federal Job Corps Centers.

17.   NAICS code 115310 – Support Activities for Forestry – Forest Fire Suppression and Fuels Management Services are two components of Support Activities for Forestry. Forest Fire Suppression includes establishments which provide services to fight forest fires. These firms usually have fire-fighting crews and equipment. Fuels Management Services firms provide services to clear land of hazardous materials that would fuel forest fires. The treatments used by these firms may include prescribed fire, mechanical removal, establishing fuel breaks, thinning, pruning, and piling.

18.   NAICS code 541519 – An Information Technology Value Added Reseller provides a total solution to information technology acquisitions by providing multi-vendor hardware and software along with significant services. Significant value added services consist of, but are not limited to, configuration consulting and design, systems integration, installation of multi-vendor computer equipment, customization of hardware or software, training, product technical support, maintenance, and end user support. For purposes of Government procurement, an information technology procurement classified under this industry category must consist of at least 15% and not more than 50% of value added services as measured by the total price less

the cost of information technology hardware, computer software, and profit. If the contract consists of less than 15% of value added services, then it must be classified under a NAICS manufacturing industry. If the contract consists of more than 50% of value added services, then it must be classified under the NAICS industry that best describes the predominate service of the procurement. To qualify as an Information Technology Value Added Reseller for purposes of SBA assistance, other than for Government procurement, a concern must be primarily engaged in providing information technology equipment and computer software and provide value added services which account for at least 15% of its receipts but not more than 50% of its receipts.

19.   NAICS Sector 92 – Small business size standards are not established for this sector. Establishments in the Public Administration sector are Federal, State, and local government agencies which administer and oversee government programs and activities that are not performed by private establishments. Concerns performing operational services for the administration of a government program are classified under the NAICS private sector industry based on the activities performed. Similarly, procurements for these types of services are classified under the NAICS private sector industry that best describes the activities to be performed. For example, if a government agency issues a procurement for law enforcement services, the requirement would be classified using one of the NAICS industry codes under NAICS industry 56161, Investigation, Guard, and Armored Car Services.

Contacts

SBA's Office of Government Contracting has six offices with an employee designated as a Size Specialist. Below are the office addresses and telephone numbers.

Area I Office of Government Contracting **Boston Area Office** U.S. Small Business Administration 10 Causeway Street Room 265 Boston, MA 02222-1093 Tel: (617) 565-5622	**Area IV** Office of Government Contracting **Chicago Area Office** U.S. Small Business Administration 500 West Madison Street Suite 1250 Chicago, IL 60661-2511 Tel: 312.353.7674
Area II Office of Government Contracting **Philadelphia Area Office** U.S. Small Business Administration Parkview Tower 1150 First Avenue Suite 1001 King of Prussia, PA 19406 Tel: (610) 382-3190	**Area V** Office Government Contracting **Dallas Area Office** U.S. Small Business Administration 4300 Amon Carter Boulevard, Suite 116 Fort Worth, TX 76155 Tel: (817) 684-5303
Area III Office of Government Contracting **Atlanta Area Office** U.S. Small Business Administration 233 Peachtree Street, NE Suite 1805 Atlanta, GA 30309 Tel: (404) 331-7587	**Area VI** Office of Government Contracting **San Francisco Area Office** U.S. Small Business Administration 455 Market Street 6th Floor San Francisco, CA 94105 Tel: (415) 744-8429

IN WASHINGTON, DC, THERE ARE TWO OFFICES THAT YOU MAY CONTACT

Office of Size Standards U.S. Small Business Administration 409 3rd Street, SW Washington, DC 20416 Tel: (202) 205-6618	**Office of Contracting Assistance** U.S. Small Business Administration 409 3rd Street, SW Washington, DC 20416 Tel: (202) 205-6460